ISBN: 178361143X

This is a **FLAME TREE NOTEBOOK**
Designed, published and © copyright 2014 Flame Tree Publishing Ltd
Based on an original image by lineartestpilot/Shutterstock.com

Flower Skull in colour • ISBN 978-1-78361-143-0

FLAME TREE PUBLISHING LIMITED
Crabtree Hall, Crabtree Lane, London SW6 6TY, United Kingdom
www.flametreepublishing.com